MAKING
WEDDING
CARDS

MAKING
WEDDING
CARDS

Over 20 easy projects for a special wedding greeting

Consultant Editor: Anke Ueberberg

NEW
HOLLAND

Published in 2005 by
New Holland Publishers (UK) Ltd.
London • Cape Town • Sydney • Auckland

Garfield House
86–88 Edgware Road
London W2 2EA
United Kingdom
www.newhollandpublishers.com

80 McKenzie Street
Cape Town 8001
South Africa

14 Aquatic Drive
Frenchs Forest, NSW 2086
Australia

218 Lake Road
Northcote, Auckland
New Zealand

ISBN 1 84330 905 X

Editor: Gareth Jones
Editorial Direction: Rosemary Wilkinson
Photographer: Shona Wood
Design: Axis Design Editions Ltd.
Template Illustration: Stephen Dew
Production: Hazel Kirkman

1 3 5 7 9 10 8 6 4 2

Reproduction by Pica Digital PTE Ltd., Singapore
Printed and bound by Times Offset (M) Sdn Bhd, Malaysia

Note
The author and publishers have made every effort to ensure that all instructions
given in this book are safe and accurate, but they cannot accept liability for any
resulting injury or loss or damage to either property or person, whether direct
or consequential and howsoever arising.

Acknowledgements
Special thanks to Fiskars UK Ltd. (Newlands Avenue, Bridgend, Wales CF31 2XA) for
supplying equipment for use in this book.

CONTENTS

My first wedding greetings card was one very similar to the acetate confetti card on page 56. The couple's invitation used subtle shades of yellow and orange, so I picked up the colour scheme and used yellow and orange confetti, with a good sprinkling of royal blue. It's a simple enough design, and can easily be personalized.

Each couple – and each occasion – is different: traditional or modern, newly-wed or married for a quarter-century. There are cards here for all of them, from the classic gold and lace combination on page 48 to the pop-up wedding cake on page 71, along with cards that can also be used as "keep the date" cards, invitations, and thank-yous, such as the double border gatefold card on page 42. The projects use a variety of techniques, including collage, iris folding, stamping and stitching, using materials such as buttons, beads, fabrics and feathers. There are simple designs here and a few that require a little bit more time. Each card can be adapted: just change the colour scheme, paper texture or pattern used to die-cut a border.

A handmade wedding card is a small gift in itself – you only need to spend a little time to make a unique card that the recipients will treasure and keep along with the other reminders of the special day.

Anke Ueberberg

GETTING STARTED

This chapter describes the tools and techniques used to make the cards in this book. Once you have mastered a few of the projects, you may want to be creative and adapt them, using the materials and paper you have, as well as the exciting odds and ends you will find once you start looking! You can keep a special "card" box and, as you discover things, store them there, so that you have all your treasures in one place.

Paper and craft shops will stock most of the things you need. The basic tools and equipment are listed in this section, but make sure you check the "you will need" list for each card before you get down to business.

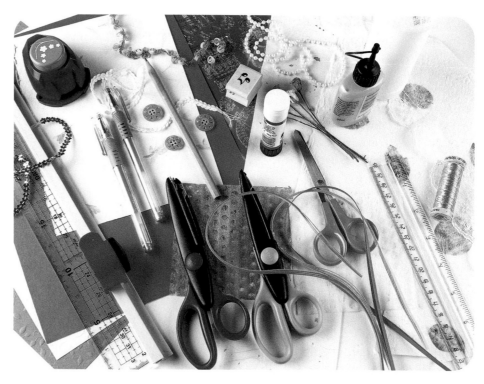

PAPER & CARD

PAPER AND CARDBOARD: When buying paper and card the abbreviations "mic" and "gsm" refer to the various thicknesses and weights of the papers and cardboards. The abbreviation "mic" is used when describing thickness and is short for microns, i.e. 1000 microns equals 1mm. The abbreviation "gsm" is used when describing the weight and is short for grams per square metre, i.e. a piece of 100gsm paper measuring 1m² weighs 100 grams. A good weight to use is 230–260gsm as this will be easy to fold but, at the same time, will not be too flimsy.

SUGAR PAPER: This paper is thick, with a slight texture, and is very reasonably priced. Because it is relatively cheap, it is a good paper to practise on, but you will need to use a double layer if you want it to be a card base.

HANDMADE PAPERS: Handmade papers are widely available in good stationery shops, artists' supply and crafts shops. There is a huge variety of colours and textures available, and you can also choose between paper with inclusions or without, and translucent or opaque paper. Of course you can also make your own handmade paper.

TISSUE PAPER: This paper comes in a range of colours, and is good to print or stencil on but is too flimsy to be used as a card blank, unless backed with something more substantial.

OTHER PAPERS: Holographic card, metallic-effect paper and card, pearlescent paper, textured and corrugated card, and a range of all kinds of other materials can be obtained from general and specialist stationery shops and artists' suppliers. Glitter-effect papers sometimes have a self-adhesive backing. Some high-street chains also offer pre-packaged selections of funky papers and card.

PAPER SIZES: Standard sizes used in this book are A4 (210 x 297mm/8¼ x 11¹¹⁄₁₆ in) and A5 (148 x 210mm/5¹³⁄₁₆ x 8¼in). A sheet of A5, when folded in half, will give you the standard size greetings card to fit into a C6 envelope. Sheets of paper and card can be bought in larger sizes (A1 or A2) from specialist paper suppliers and cut to suit your requirements.

PENS, PENCILS & PAINTS

FELT TIPS, MARKERS AND GEL PENS:
These are available in every colour you can
think of, and a range of tip sizes. They are
useful for everything from decorating
borders to writing messages.

SILVER AND GOLD MARKER PENS:
Metallic colours look great on both light
and dark backgrounds.

PENCILS: Pencils must be kept sharp for
accurate marking. An HB pencil is a good
hard pencil for marking edges to be cut –
use a softer pencil, such as a 2B, if you
think you are going to make mistakes or
need to rub the line out. A good eraser
is also important for this reason.

PAINT: A selection of watercolour and
acrylic paints is also useful. Metallic acrylic
colours come in a variety of shades –
choose the more glittery ones for best
effect. Always use good quality paint brushes
– they will not leave hairs on the paper
after painting.

CUTTING & SCORING EQUIPMENT

CUTTING MAT: If you use cardboard for
cutting on, it retains score marks from a
craft knife or scalpel, so it will need to be
changed frequently. Using a cutting mat is
much easier as it self-seals so your craft
knife will not get stuck in previous score
marks. The cutting mat allows the blade to
sink into the material while cutting through
the paper or card.

CRAFT KNIFE: A good, sharp craft knife
is essential to keep your cut edges neat,
so you may need to change your blade
frequently. This also eliminates torn edges
resulting from cutting paper with a blunt
knife. Most craft knives come with blades
which you can snap off when they become
blunt. Scalpels can also be used – these are
very sharp, so be very careful and have a

supply of spare blades to hand if you
are going to be doing a lot of cutting.
*It is very important to take great care when
cutting – never cut towards your body. Have
plasters handy just in case!*

SCISSORS: Do not use scissors reserved
for cutting fabric on paper or card as the
paper will blunt the blades. It is handy to
have a couple of different sizes of scissors –
a large pair for general work and a small
pair, like nail scissors, for fiddly detail.
Pattern-edge scissors can create amazing
effects. Be careful when lining up the
pattern from cut to cut. A pair of scissors
with a smaller pattern can be used for
details and a larger pattern for more
dramatic results.

RULERS: A metal ruler is a good edge to
cut against. If you haven't got a metal ruler,
it will be worth investing in one, as the
blade on a craft knife can cut into the
surface of a plastic ruler and ruin your
work. A paper guillotine is also useful, but
not essential, as is a set square, to help
you cut accurate right angles.

ADHESIVES

You will need a range of different glues for different purposes:

PVA ADHESIVE: This is a strong glue which forms a permanent bond when used on paper and board. It dries leaving a transparent finish.

GLUE STICKS: You can buy glue sticks with a fine tip which can be useful for writing. Glitter or embossing powder can be sprinkled over the glue.

GLITTER GLUE: This also comes in different thicknesses and many different colours. A fine tip applicator makes it easy to write out greetings.

SPRAY ADHESIVE: This is commonly used for sticking paper to paper or board as it has the great virtue of sticking firmly. Re-positioning can be possible for up to 30 seconds after bonding two surfaces. Always protect the area surrounding the paper or object you are spraying with some newspaper. Spraying into a box is a good way of protecting surfaces. Remember to use in a well-ventilated room and carefully read the instructions on the can!

ALL-PURPOSE CLEAR ADHESIVE: This is a strong, cement-like adhesive used for sticking objects together. It is ideal for mixed media and fabric and dries leaving a transparent finish.

STICKY TAPE: Cellophane tape, masking tape, doubled-sided tape, magic tape, sticky fixers and foam pads are all useful. Double-sided tape can be used as an alternative to glue when you are working with the more lightweight craft materials. Masking tape can be useful when spraying glue on specific areas of a card or blocking out certain colours when colouring. Sticky fixing foam pads can be used as an adhesive and also create a 3D effect.

COCKTAIL STICKS/COTTON BUDS: These are very handy for applying glue to small or fiddly items.

OTHER STUFF

STAMPS: Stamps can be bought in all manner of shapes and sizes from shops or by mail order from specialist stamp manufacturers. Ink pads come in all the colours of the rainbow as well as in gold, silver and bronze. Special embossing ink pads can be used in conjunction with embossing powder to create a raised effect when the embossing powder is heated to melting point. When using stamps for decorating a card, make sure they are evenly covered with stamping ink.

PUNCHES: These come in a range of shapes and patterns, and are used to make delicate cut-out motifs in paper and card. The punched-out bits can also be used for decorating the front of the cards or on gift tags and envelopes.

SEWING EQUIPMENT: Different sized needles are useful for a variety of sewing effects. Threads can also be bought in different thicknesses. A thimble is handy for protecting your thumb or fingers when sewing through thick card.

TWEEZERS: Use tweezers to pick up and move smaller items such as quilled elements, or confetti.

PRECISION HEAT TOOL: A heat tool is necessary to activate and fix embossing powder. These tools get extremely hot, so you must be careful when using them, keeping your hands and the paper or card that is being heated a safe distance away from the heat source. Always follow the manufacturer's instructions.

PERGAMANO PERFORATING TOOLS: These include 1-, 2-, 3-, 4- and 5-needle tools, a 7-needle or flower tool and a semi-circle tool.

"EXCELLENT" PERFORATING PAD: This is a black synthetic pad on which to perforate your patterns.

PERGAMANO EMBOSSING TOOLS: There are a number of these, including fine stylus, extra fine, small and large ball, and a hockeystick-shaped tool.

PERGAMANO EMBOSSING PADS: These include a small blue pad, "De Luxe" and "King-Size" black pads.

GLITTER AND CONFETTI: Glitter and confetti is available in a range of shapes and colours and is available from many card and stationery shops. It can be stuck onto cards or dropped into the envelope as a surprise.

COLLECTIBLES: Lace, shells, coins, old photographs and postcards, stamps, buttons, ribbons, raffia, feathers and much more can be found in flea markets, charity shops, haberdashery shops or even your home.

Keep all of these things in labelled bags or envelopes, where necessary, to make life easier. Similarly, make a file for magazine cuttings, wrapping paper and pieces of handmade paper.

CARD MAKING TECHNIQUES

CUTTING AND SCORING: You will need
a craft knife, steel ruler and cutting mat to
score or cut medium-weight cardboard or
thick paper. First, take the card and cut it
to the desired size using a set square and
ruler to make sure the corners are square.
On the outside of the cardboard, measure
the centre line where the card will fold
and mark it with a pencil. Make sure the
pencil mark is parallel to the edge, or the
card will not fold properly. Then, using the
metal ruler and craft knife, lightly score
over the pencil line but make sure only to
score the top layer of the cardboard with
your craft knife.

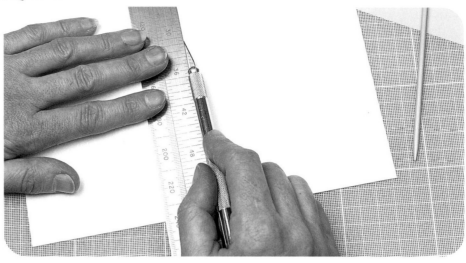

CUTTING A WINDOW: Use a ruler to
measure the centre of the front of the card
and mark lightly with a pencil. Then, using
a set square, mark out where you wish to
have the window, using the centre mark
as a guide. Check the window is centred
correctly by using a ruler to measure from
the edge of the card to the edge of the
window. With the card opened flat on a
cutting mat, carefully cut out the window
using a ruler and sharp craft knife. Move
the card around when cutting each edge so
you are always cutting parallel to (and never
towards) your body. Cut with the window
on the inside of the rule, so you can see
where the pencil lines begin and end. Take
care not to extend the cuts beyond the
corners of the window.

TORN EDGES: An attractive finish to
your card or the design within your card
is a torn edge, which is a characteristic of
many handmade and water-colour papers.
To achieve this effect, measure and mark
with a pencil where you wish the torn edge
to be. Fold the paper over along this line so
that you have a crease to work with. Firmly
hold down the ruler against the crease and
tear the paper by pulling away or towards
you. Do a little at a time and press the ruler
down firmly to avoid ripping the paper
where you don't want it to tear.

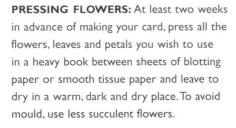

RUNNING STITCH: Bring the needle and thread up through the fabric or material to the right side, then insert the needle further along the material in a straight line parallel to the edge. Leave a smaller gap on the wrong side before bringing the thread up on the right side again and repeat the process to create a running stitch.

PRESSING FLOWERS: At least two weeks in advance of making your card, press all the flowers, leaves and petals you wish to use in a heavy book between sheets of blotting paper or smooth tissue paper and leave to dry in a warm, dark and dry place. To avoid mould, use less succulent flowers.

PERGAMANO EMBOSSING: In this instance, "embossing" means raising parts of the design by rubbing the reverse side with a metal tool. The paper fibres are stretched and compressed by the pressure of the tool and the natural light grey colour of the Pergamano parchment paper will change to satin white. Applying soft pressure results in a half tone of white, and higher pressure produces a proper white tone. By changing the intensity of the pressure applied you can achieve a mixture of tones.

PERGAMANO PERFORATING: The perforations are often made into Pergamano parchment paper, along borders, either with the pattern underneath or over a special metal grid. The dots on the patterns or the openings in the metal grid show where to perforate. These needles are sharp, so take extra care when you are using them.

MAKING ENVELOPES

Although most of the projects are a suitable size for commercially available envelopes, it is often more appropriate to create a matching envelope for a handmade card.

Making an envelope is a fairly easy task and the advantage of a homemade envelope is that you can design it so that it will co-ordinate with your card.

you will need

- sheet of paper approximately three times the width of your card
- scissors
- pencil
- metal ruler
- glue stick

1 Place the greetings card centrally on the bottom edge of the sheet of paper. Fold the sheet of paper down over the greetings card. Open up the sheet of paper.

2 Place the card along the fold line you have just created. Fold the paper up over the greetings card (it should cover the card). Next, fold the paper down over the greetings card.

3 Open up both folds. Next fold the side sections of paper inwards over the card. Open up the two new folds. You should now have four fold lines.

4 Place the sheet of paper onto a cutting board, and, using a craft knife and metal ruler, cut away the four rectangular sections marked by the fold lines in each corner of the sheet of paper. You should be left with two large flaps on either side of the central section. These flaps will become your tabs.

5 Use the pencil to mark up 1cm (½in) wide tabs on each of the flaps. Use the craft knife to trim away the excess paper.

6 Fold the lower section of the envelope upwards and use a glue stick to stick the tabs down over what will form the back of the envelope. When you have placed the greetings card in the envelope, fold the upper back of the envelope down over the card and use a glue stick to seal your envelope.

PACKING AND PADDING: Each week a huge number of cards travel through the post and via courier companies. Often the outside packaging gets damaged, so it is important to ensure that the more delicate your card is, the more protection you give it. Nothing is more heartbreaking than to make and send a beautiful card only to find it was damaged by the time it got to its destination. Gift-wrap your creation with tissue paper or cellophane to make it extra special, then send in a padded or stiff-backed envelope.

DECORATING ENVELOPES: You can personalize envelopes in many ways. Make one yourself from beautiful textured, handmade paper; wax-seal your envelopes; wrap the finished card and envelope in contrasting tissue or crepe paper and tie with gold cord; or embellish your envelope flap with small decorative elements from the card inside.

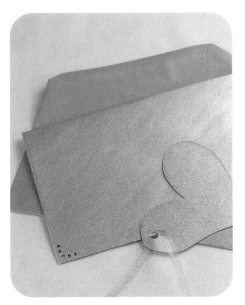

GIFT TAGS: If you have left-over card, fabric, paper or other material from making a card, why not create a matching gift tag? You can also adapt elements of many of the projects in this book to a much smaller format and use them as gift tags.

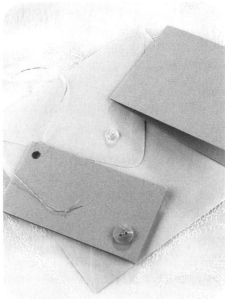

Here is an overview of the wide range of card designs to choose from in the projects section.

There are cards here that will cover every kind of wedding occasion – from "keep the date" and invitations to wedding and anniversary congratulations and thank-you cards, with tips on adapting the designs and advice on gift tags and envelopes.

Woven Ribbon p.17

Rose Petal Squares p.20

Nine Petal Hearts p.22

The Happy Couple p.24

The Big Day p.27

Rose Fabric Collage p.30

Triple Heart Concertina p.32

Lace & Ribbon Roses p.35

Embossed Heart p.38

Pergamano Hearts p.40

Double Border Gatefold p.42

Cherubs & Hearts p.44

Rose Panel Card p.46

Gold & Lace p.48

Pergamano Rings p.50

Pink Pearl & Organza p.53

Acetate Confetti p.56

Wedding Cake p.58

Champagne Occasion p.60

Organza Confetti Bag p.63

Net & Wedding Confetti p.66

Petal Paper Wallet p.68

Pop-up Cake p.71

WOVEN RIBBON

This woven ribbon heart in delicate creams, pinks and greens is bordered with a cotton lace frill and set in heavy watercolour paper. Spray adhesives and the wide range of ribbons available make this a relatively simple and effective card to make.

you will need

- A5 sheet of pink card
- cutting mat
- soft pencil and metal ruler
- set square
- craft knife
- eraser
- sheet of lightweight paper
- spray adhesive
- selection of narrow ribbons in pink, green and cream
- scissors
- heavy watercolour paper
- Woven Ribbon template (page 77)
- tracing paper
- 35cm (13¾in) length of narrow cotton lace
- needle
- white thread
- glue stick

1 Take the A5 sheet of pink card. Measure and cut out a rectangle 10.5 x 21cm (4¼ x 8¼in). Measure halfway along the long edges, top and bottom. Score the card and fold it in half. Erase any pencil marks that remain.

2 Take the sheet of lightweight paper and spray a 10 x 20cm (4 x 8in) area with the spray adhesive. Allow it to become tacky. Place 15cm (6in) lengths of ribbon, one beside the other, across the paper, to a depth of 9cm (3½in).

3 Lift up every other length of ribbon, starting with the second strip, and fold it back. Place a length of ribbon vertically then lie the horizontal ribbons back in place.

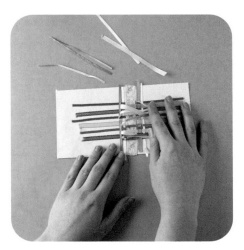

4 Now lift up every other length of ribbon, this time starting with the first strip, and repeat the process with another vertical length of ribbon. Continue this until you have covered an area at least 9cm (3½in) square.

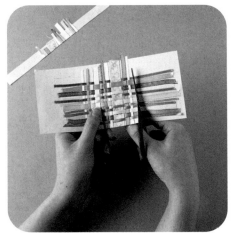

5 When you have made a woven square of ribbon, press the ribbons down firmly on the card so they don't lift up. Then trim the card to a 9cm (3½in) square.

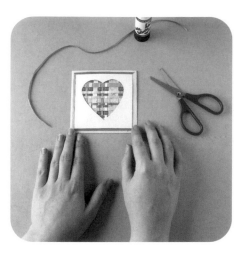

6 Cut a 9cm (3½in) square of watercolour paper. Trace the template and cut it out. Place the heart shape centrally on the square of watercolour paper and draw around it.

7 Cut out the heart shape using the craft knife.

8 Glue the square of ribbon weaving centrally onto the card blank and glue the heart frame on top of that. Glue a pink ribbon border to the watercolour paper.

9 Finally, sew a running stitch along the length of lace. Gently pull the thread to gather up the lace and attach as a border around the ribbon heart with the glue stick.

variations & extras

You can adapt the size and shape of the woven ribbon design as you wish. Smaller shapes are ideal for stylish gift tags.

ROSE PETAL SQUARES

Delicate textures and patterns contrast well with the vibrant pink in this card – not a colour for the faint-hearted! This card works best when cut and interleaved accurately for a professional look.

you will need

- sheet of rose petal handmade paper (choose your sheet carefully – see step 1)
- cutting mat
- metal ruler
- craft knife
- Japanese-style pink tissue paper (i.e. thin and lacy with faint pattern)
- pattern-stitched pink paper
- glue stick
- 12 x 24cm (4¾ x 9½in) piece of plain white card
- 11 x 23cm (4⅜ x 9in) piece of silver paper

tip

For a more subtle appearance, replace the bright pink strips with pastel pink translucent paper, or use different petal paper with matching colour strips.

1 On the rose petal paper, look for two petals approximately 5cm (2in) apart. Cut out a 4 x 12cm (1½ x 4¾in) strip with the two rose petals at either end, two 4 x 12cm (1½ x 4¾in) strips with single petals in the middle of each strip, one 4 x 12cm (1½ x 4¾in) strip of Japanese tissue paper, and two 4 x 12cm (1½ x 4¾in) strips of pattern-stitched paper.

2 Lay the two single-petal strips of paper parallel to each other, 4cm (1½in) apart. Apply glue stick to one end of both strips and position one of the strips of pattern-stitched pink paper precisely at 90° across them to make a U-shape. Then repeat at the other end of the single petal strips with the second pattern-stitched pink strip.

3 Glue the two-petal strip on top of the pattern-stitched paper between the other two petal strips. Weigh the panel down under a book for at least 10 minutes. Weave the Japanese-style tissue paper in from the underside, across the central square and back down, then glue on to the underside.

4 Score and fold the plain white card down the middle. Fold the inlay paper in half, silver side in. Apply a thin line of glue on one side of the fold line of the silver inlay and stick the inlay down on the right-hand side of the white card's fold line.

5 Apply the glue stick along the edges and the centre of the front of the white card and stick down the pink-and-petal panel. Weigh the card down under a heavy book for at least 10 minutes – the longer the better, to ensure that the card stays flat.

NINE PETAL HEARTS

The number nine signifies "forever" or "eternity" in Chinese culture and is considered auspicious for celebrations. Red roses are a traditional western gift of love, making this a perfect wedding card.

you will need

- a minimum of 9 pressed red rose petals
- 2 sheets of blotting paper
- 9 sheets of mulberry paper in pink, lilac, purple, dark green, turquoise, earth green, yellow, orange, dark orange
- cocktail stick
- PVA glue
- A5 sheet of textured white card, folded in half
- scissors

tip

The torn paper squares should butt up against each other, but make sure you do not overlap them or the separate colours will not stand out so well.

1 Two weeks in advance, press the rose petals between the sheets of blotting paper in the pages of a heavy book and leave them to dry out completely in a warm, dark and dry place.

2 Measure and fold a 3cm (1¼in) square on one of the sheets of mulberry paper, then tear along the folds to make a rough-edged square. Repeat with each of the different colours.

3 Using a cocktail stick, apply PVA glue to the back of one of the squares of mulberry paper and stick it to the top left-hand corner of the front of the folded white card about 1cm (⅜in) from each edge. Stick down the rest of the squares close to each other to form a 9cm (3½in) multicolour square.

4 Using the scissors, carefully cut each pressed rose petal into a heart shape that will fit the 3cm (1¼in) squares of paper.

5 Apply glue to the back of the petal and stick to the middle of the top left coloured square. Repeat until all the squares are filled.

THE HAPPY COUPLE

Iris-folding looks very sophisticated but is quite easy to do. It works particularly well with a varied selection of papers. This diamond-shape iris is perfect as a frame for the happy couple.

you will need

- 15.5 x 32.5cm (6⅛ x 12¾in) piece of ivory card
- cutting mat
- soft pencil and metal ruler
- craft knife
- eraser
- 2 photocopies of The Happy Couple template (page 74)
- selection of 12 gold-tone and 12 red-tone paper strips, each 2 x 10cm (¾ x 4in)
- adhesive tape
- glue stick
- 14 x 20.5cm (5½ x 8⅛in) piece of pearlescent ivory paper
- wedding couple stamp (check the stamp fits inside the centre square of the iris template, approximately 3cm (1¼in) square)
- gold daubing stick or stamp pad

tip

Pre-cut the tape strips and stick them to the edge of the cutting mat so they are handy when you need to secure the paper strips.

1 Place the ivory card face down on the cutting mat and, working from the left, measure and mark along the long edges, top and bottom, at 10.5cm (4¼in) and 21cm (8¼in). Score between these marks to make two folds. Erase any pencil marks that remain.

2 On the middle panel, measure and mark halfway between the two score lines on the top and bottom edges and draw a vertical line between the two marks. Then, working from the top edge, measure down both lines and mark at 7cm (2¾in), then draw a horizontal line between the two marks.

3 Cut out the first of the two templates and align the four corners so that two touch the horizontal pencil line and the other two touch the vertical line. Mark where the corners touch the lines, and carefully cut out the resulting diamond shape. Erase the remaining pencil marks.

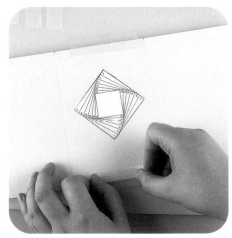

4 Trim around the second template, leaving a wide margin of paper around the outside. Stick the template on to the cutting mat with the adhesive tape. Place the card on top, face down, with the diamond-shaped window exactly over the template. Lightly secure with tape.

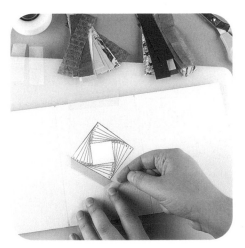

5 Fold the first strip of the gold-tone paper in half along its width, and place on top of the area marked 1 on the template, fold facing towards the centre. Secure both ends of the paper strip with tape, trimming it to ensure it doesn't cross either of the score lines.

6 Following number order on the template, continue sticking down strips, alternating between the red- and gold-tone papers, securing them with tape as in step 5. Make sure that facing strips match each other (i.e. use the same paper for 1 and 3, 2 and 4, 5 and 7, 6 and 8 etc.).

7 Once you have stuck down paper strips over all of the numbers on the template, fully secure the ends with long strips of tape. Then carefully detach the tape securing the card and lift the card away from the template.

8 Fold over the left-hand panel. Turn the card over with the neat side of the iris window facing you, and, with the pencil, lightly mark the shape of the square iris window onto the panel beneath.

9 Unfold and cut out the square on the left-hand panel. Apply glue stick to the left-hand and middle panels, then stick the left-hand panel to the middle panel, over the taped-down paper strips. Press down firmly.

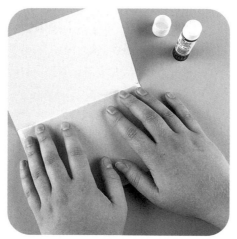

10 Fold the pearlescent paper in half, apply a thin line of glue on one side of the fold line and stick this down to the left of the central fold of the card. Weigh the card down under a heavy book for a minimum of 30 minutes – the longer the better, as the card will be a little bulky.

11 Check the wedding couple stamp to make sure it fits the iris. Ink the stamp pad and carefully stamp onto the inlay paper through the centre square of the iris. (If you are at all worried about accuracy, mark the inside of the panel through the iris with the pencil, then open the card, stamp inside the square, and erase the pencil lines.)

Romantic pastel colours, golden hearts and a gold embossed stamp neatly enfold a gift of flower petal confetti. This card would also make a lovely wedding invitation or "keep the date" card.

you will need

- A4 sheet of white textured card
- cutting mat
- soft pencil and metal ruler
- craft knife
- eraser
- pastel pink handmade paper
- paint brush and water
- iron and ironing board
- glue stick
- stamp with a romantic image
- embossing stamp pad
- gold embossing powder
- precision heat tool
- gold foil hearts
- tweezers
- gold outliner
- 10 x 12cm (4 x 4¾in) piece of white mulberry paper
- hole punch
- suitable dried flower petals
- short length of narrow pale pink ribbon

1 Cut the A4 sheet of paper in half. Taking one of the halves, score and fold in half again. Using a ruler and the lightest of pencil marks, measure a rectangle 9 x 13cm (3½ x 5⅛in) onto the handmade paper.

2 Using the paint brush, generously dipped in water, paint a water line around the marked-out rectangle, thoroughly soaking the paper.

3 Carefully tear the rectangle out. Set an iron to medium heat and iron the paper dry. Allow the paper to cool, then use the glue stick to attach it centrally to the card blank.

4 Using your chosen stamp, print the image using an embossing stamp pad onto the other half of the textured card. You may wish to print several images, then choose the best.

5 Sprinkle the gold embossing powder over the stamped image. Shake any excess powder onto a scrap of paper and return it to the pot.

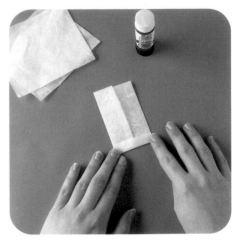

6 Carefully set the embossed image using the heat tool. Then cut out the image leaving a narrow border around it.

7 Use the glue stick to attach the embossed picture to the card. Once the glue has set, decorate the card with gold foil hearts: pick them up with tweezers, dab them onto the glue stick and place on the card. Frame the embossed image with the gold outliner.

8 To make the bag of confetti, fold the two sides of the mulberry paper into the centre so they overlap slightly and fold up the base. Then glue the edges in place.

9 Emboss the image on the front of the bag and use a hole punch to make two small holes for the ribbon tie. Fill the bag with flower petals. Thread the ribbon through the holes, tie a bow and use a small dab of glue to attach inside the card.

variations & extras
Use your chosen stamp to co-ordinate the envelope or gift tag accompanying the card.

ROSE FABRIC COLLAGE

The strongly coloured card contrasts well with the delicate rose pattern
fabric used here. The fringe adds an element of movement – cut it straight
as shown here, or use saw-toothed fabric scissors for a different effect.

you will need

- A5 piece of duo-tone red/pink or red card
- cutting mat
- soft pencil and metal ruler
- craft knife or scoring tool
- 14.5 x 20cm (5¾ x 8in) piece of cream inlay paper
- eraser
- 2 pieces of fabric with different rose patterns, approximately 10cm (4in) square and 7cm (2¾in) square
- iron and ironing board
- sharp pair of scissors
- glue stick

tip

Quilting fabric is a good source of different rose patterns.

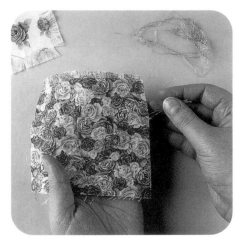

1 Mark, score and fold the red card in half, red side out. Next, score fold the cream paper in half for the inlay. Erase any remaining pencil marks.

2 Iron the fabric pieces on a very low setting if they are not completely flat. Pull out individual threads on the sides of the pieces of fabric to make a fringe of approximately 1cm (⅜in). For the larger fabric panel, the "solid" area should be about 7.5 x 8cm (3 x 3⅛in) and about 4.5 x 5cm (1¾ x 2in) for the smaller one.

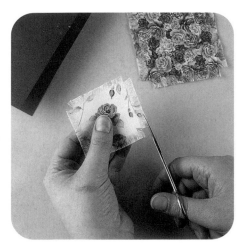

3 Trim the fringe of the larger piece to straighten it all around and position it on the card to check that it fits. Trim the fringe of the smaller piece to just under 1cm (⅜in) and position on the larger piece, leaving a small margin. Trim the fringes further, if necessary.

4 Apply a thin line of glue next to the fold of the inlay paper and glue down to the right of the score line on the inside of the red card. Make sure it is centred between the top and bottom.

5 Carefully apply glue stick to the back of the bigger fabric panel, taking care not to pull out further threads. Position the panel and smoothe down on the front of the card. Glue the smaller panel onto the centre of the larger panel and gently "comb" the fringe with your fingers. Weigh the card down under a book for at least half an hour.

TRIPLE **HEART** CONCERTINA

This simple and stylish card is easy to make yet very effective, with a small flourish of sequins and beads to add movement. Use gold instead of silver card for a more traditional look.

you will need

- A4 sheet of silver card, with a white back
- cutting mat
- soft pencil and metal ruler
- craft knife
- eraser
- photocopy of Triple Heart Concertina template (page 74)
- scissors
- short piece of silver flower sequin strip with the sequins undone, or a few loose sequins
- long silver or glass beads
- silver thread
- beading needle
- Fiskars heart corner punch

tip

Unless you are confident about using the craft knife to cut out the curves of the hearts, use a pair of sharp scissors.

1 Lay the card silver-side down on the cutting mat and, from the left, mark along the long edges, top and bottom, at one third and two thirds of the total length. Score vertically between the marks. Erase any pencil marks that remain.

2 Cut out the template of the heart and the inside of the heart shape. Place the heart onto the left-hand panel of the card, at a slight angle, making sure the two cheeks of the heart are touching either side of the panel, and the top edge is about 5cm (2in) from the top edge of the card.

3 Once in position, draw around the top edge of the heart from where it meets the left edge of the card to the first fold line, then draw around the inside. Repeat for the middle panel, with the top edge of the heart 2.5cm (1in) from the top edge of the card. Repeat for the final panel, with the top edge of the heart touching the top edge of the card.

4 Fold the card along the score lines to create the concertina fold (i.e with the silver side of the left-hand panel at the front). Unfold, and lay silver-side down on the cutting mat. Cut carefully around the top of each heart outline until you reach either a fold line or the edge of the card.

5 Align the metal ruler along the first score line and cut from where one heart shape meets the fold to where the score line meets the next heart shape. Do the same on the next score line.

6 Now carefully cut around the inside of the heart shapes. Use the eraser to remove any pencil marks that remain. Smoothe down the cut edges on both sides of the card, then re-fold.

7 For the bead-and-flower strip, thread five beads and five flower sequins, starting with a bead and alternating between beads and flowers, then backtrack with the needle, always going along the other side of the sequin and through the bead.

8 Make a small hole in the top bow of the front heart shape with the needle. Thread the bead-and-flower strip through from the front, then make a double knot of the two ends of the strip at the back and trim.

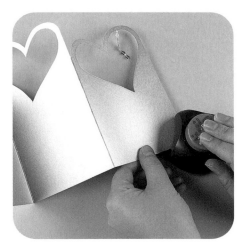

9 Finally, carefully use the corner punch to decorate the front and back corners of the card.

extras

Use the corner punch to decorate the envelope. The heart cut-outs make excellent gift tags: erase any pencil marks, hole-punch and thread with matching ribbon.

LACE & RIBBON ROSES

This pretty card has an old-fashioned charm about it, while still looking fresh and delicate. You could use a different colour scheme: for example, a light orange ribbon and yellow roses on ivory paper.

you will need

- 13.5 x 29cm (5¼ x 11½in) piece of very pale lilac textured or plain card
- cutting mat
- soft pencil and metal ruler
- craft knife or scoring tool
- eraser
- cocktail stick
- PVA glue
- 15cm (6in) length of 4cm (1½in) wide lilac or purple ribbon
- 15cm (6in) length of 3cm (1¼in) wide lace
- 15cm (6in) length of 0.5cm (¼in) wide purple velvet ribbon
- glue stick
- 5 ribbon roses
- 13 x 17cm (5⅛ x 6¾in) piece of magenta paper, folded in half, for the inlay

tip

Make sure the ribbon and lace strips are completely flat – iron them on a very low setting if they are not.

1 Lay the card textured-side down on the cutting mat and, from the left, measure and mark along the long edges, top and bottom at 9cm (3½in), 14.5cm (5¾in), 15.5cm (6⅛in) and 20cm (8in), and score. Erase any remaining pencil marks.

2 Fold inwards along the score line at 14.5cm (5¾in), and outwards along the score line at 15.5cm (6⅛in), to create a "lip". The edge of the panel to the right (between fold lines at 15.5cm (6⅛in) and 20cm (8in)) should now sit on top of the panel to the left (between fold lines at 9cm (3½in) and 14.5cm (5¾in)).

3 Turn the card over, and, using the cocktail stick, apply a thin line of PVA along the side of the fold beneath the lip. Position the lilac ribbon along this fold and press down gently.

4 Apply a thin line of glue to the edge of the ribbon under the lip and position the lace on top, up against the fold. Apply glue to the underside of the lip and press the lip down firmly. Weigh down under a heavy book for at least half an hour.

5 With the edges of ribbon and lace now well hidden under the lip, dot a thin line of PVA glue along the edge of the lip and glue down the velvet ribbon so that it hides the edge. Weigh down again under a heavy book for at least half an hour.

6 Turn the card over so the ribbon and lace are face down. Apply glue stick to the ends of the ribbon and lace, fold them over the top and bottom edges of the card and press down firmly.

7 Apply the glue stick to the left-hand panel (the panel nearest to the edge of the lilac ribbon) and fold it over the middle panels to hide the ribbon ends. Weigh the card down under a heavy book for at least half an hour.

8 Apply generous blobs of PVA glue to the back of the flowers and leave them to get tacky. Approximately 1cm (⅜in) from the left of the velvet ribbon, dot five small blobs of glue in a vertical line approximately 1.5cm (⅝in) apart, and allow to become tacky. Position the flowers and hold them in place until they stay upright.

9 Once the glue on the flowers has dried completely, fold the inlay paper in half, apply a thin line of glue on one side of the fold line and stick down to the right of the main fold.

variations & extras
You may wish to arrange the fabric roses in a little "nest" instead, undersides well tucked-in. For a gift tag, fold a 9cm (3½in) square piece of matching card in half, hole-punch in one corner and thread with velvet ribbon. Glue down a single rose on the card.

EMBOSSED **HEART**

Pink, red and gold – the luscious colours of love! Whispy handmade paper,
red and holographic gold card and the lace effect of the embossed pattern
make a splendid card to send to a couple you really adore.

you will need

- embossing stamp pad (tinted)
- rose design stamp
- A4 sheet of red card
- gold embossing powder
- precision heat tool
- Embossed Heart template (page 76)
- spray adhesive
- A5 sheet of shiny gold card
- A4 sheet of pink handmade paper
- cutting mat
- soft pencil and metal ruler
- craft knife or scoring tool
- pattern edge scissors
- 14 x 28cm (5½ x 11in) piece of white card folded in half
- all-purpose glue
- plastic jewel

1 With the rose stamp and the embossing stamp pad, stamp your design onto one half of the red card. Sprinkle the gold powder over the image before the ink dries, and shake any excess powder off into the container. Heat the image with the precision heat tool until the powder has melted.

2 Using the template, cut out a heart shape from the embossed card. Apply spray adhesive to the back and stick on to the gold card. Now cut around the heart shape, leaving a 0.5cm (¼in) gold border.

3 Cut out a square of the handmade pink paper about 0.5–1cm (¼–⅜in) larger than the heart at its widest points. Apply spray adhesive to the back of the heart shape and stick centrally onto the pink paper square.

4 Using the pattern-edge scissors, cut out a square from the left-over red card, ensuring it is 1cm (⅜in) larger all around than the pink square. Apply spray adhesive to the back of the pink paper square and stick centrally on to the red card.

5 Cut another piece of pink handmade paper slightly larger than the front of the folded white card. Glue the pink paper to the front of the card, and trim to match the edge. Finally, glue the collage to the centre of the front of the card, and fix a plastic jewel to the top of the heart with all-purpose glue.

PERGAMANOHEARTS

Using a ready-made grid under the parchment and a special perforator – the Diamond tool – you can create this lovely parchment pattern which is rather like the weave of linen.

you will need

- A4 sheet of parchment paper
- Pergamano Hearts templates (page 77)
- white 01T and gold 22T Tinta inks
- Easy-Grid template with "Excellent" pad
- "Diamond" perforating tool
- fine stylus and small ball embossing tool and pad
- 1- and 4-needle perforating tools
- hockeystick tool
- adhesive tape
- Dorso crayons, box 1
- no. 2 paintbrush
- Pergamano scissors and Perga-Soft
- 14 x 28cm (5½ x 11in) piece of pink card, folded in half

before you begin

Trace the template onto the parchment paper with Tinta white and gold. Apply Dorso magenta on the reverse side of the centres of the white outlined hearts, and emboss between the double lines.

1 Tape the parchment paper right side up on the grid, with the first heart running in line with the grid. Place the Diamond tool vertically into the grid alongside the paper. Its weight will help it find its place square on the grid. Lift the tool up, keeping it in the same position relative to the grid and move over the first white heart. Keeping the tool vertical, press lightly and evenly.

2 Perforate into every hole on the grid within the heart-shaped area. After the first heart has been perforated, release the paper, move into place for the next heart and repeat steps 1 and 2 until all the alternate hearts are perforated. Remember to use adhesive tape each time to secure the paper and to prevent it from slipping.

3 Now work on the red hearts, (note that not every hole is perforated – creating a different design). Position the paper first and follow the perforation design.

4 Once you have completed the perforation, apply white lines in a criss-cross pattern using the no. 2 brush and Tinta white.

5 With the 4-needle tool, perforate around the entire outline, starting on the line from the fold into the heart circle. Let two needles glide into the former holes so that all the perforations are equally spaced. Perforate along the second line which leads back to the fold of the card. Trim the parchment to 14 x 28cm (5½ x 11in) and insert the pink card.

DOUBLE **BORDER** GATEFOLD

The shadow effect of the border is created here by repeating it on the inlay of this subtle and sophisticated card. You can easily vary the colour scheme by changing the inlay paper.

you will need

- 12 x 24cm (4¾ x 9½in) piece of ivory card
- cutting mat
- soft pencil and metal ruler
- craft knife
- 12 x 25cm (4¾ x 9¾in) piece of pale blue translucent paper
- eraser
- Fiskars flower border punch or similar
- glue stick

tip

This card is very simple to make and would be ideal for producing multiples, for example, "keep the date" cards, invitations, or thank-you cards, with or without a printed inlay.

1 Place the ivory card face down on the cutting mat. Measure and mark along the long edges, top and bottom, at 6 and 18cm (2⅜ and 7in). Do the same for the blue translucent paper, marking it at just over 6.5 and just under 18.5cm (2½ and 7¼in), to fit inside the folded card. Score and fold, then erase any remaining pencil marks.

2 Practise cutting a continuous border with the punch. When you're confident with the tool, turn the card face up and punch a border along the short edges. Repeat on the inlay paper, but keep the blue flower shapes produced by the punch, and put them to one side.

3 Fold the card and the inlay, and smoothe the folds. Apply a thin line of glue just inside the left and right folds of the card and position the inlay precisely in the middle of the centre panel. Close the card, then press in a heavy book for a minimum of 10 minutes.

4 Decorate the finished card with the blue flower cut-outs, gluing them down with tiny dots of glue applied with the cocktail stick in a random pattern on the two gates of the ivory card. Punch some extra flower shapes from the blue translucent paper or other blue paper, as required.

variations

For an even simpler card, use handmade card or paper with petal enclosures (but note that handmade card can be a bit stiff and difficult to punch). When cutting the card make sure the gate sections have a good sprinkling of petals.

CHERUBS&HEARTS

This romantic design lends itself to weddings, but you can use any other suitable line drawing and adapt the card to suit the tastes of the bride and groom. Have a go – its easier than it looks!

you will need

- A5 sheet of red card, folded in half
- medium gauge aluminium foil, approximately 11 x 15.5cm (4⅜ x 6⅛in)
- wooden skewer
- Cherubs & Hearts template (page 75)
- scissors
- tracing paper
- PVA glue

tip

You can include a message on the card, but remember that the scoring is done from the reverse of the card, so any words will have to be written in mirror writing.

Spray the foil with gold paint for a Golden Wedding Anniversary card.

1 Place the folded card on the aluminium sheet and score around it with the point of a wooden skewer to make a rectangle approximately 10.5 x 15cm (4¼ x 6in). Press down firmly to score a clear line into the foil.

2 Using the scissors, trim off the excess foil just outside the scored outline. Take care not to cut yourself on the sharp edges of the foil.

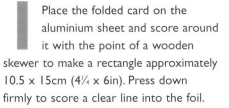

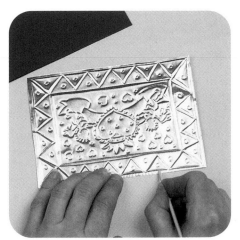

3 Inside the foil rectangle, score a smaller rectangle measuring 6.5 x 10cm (2½ x 4in) on the same (reverse) side of the foil, to create an equal border all around the card. Score a zigzag pattern within the border and add small circles inside each triangle.

4 Trace the template, then lay the tracing paper over the reverse of the foil. Using the border to position the template, score the design onto the aluminium sheet in a fluid movement. Add hearts and small circles as desired.

5 Turn the foil over, and, still using the skewer, draw along either side of any key lines of the picture again to highlight them. Score a series of short vertical lines all along the very edge of the foil to create a border decoration. Glue the foil to the front of the red card.

ROSE PANEL CARD

This rose panel card combines different textures, a flash of intense colour and 3D elements to stunning effect. This will also work well with a different colour scheme, for example pink and purple on white, or white on lime green... Give it a whirl!

you will need

- A5 sheet of white card
- cutting mat
- soft pencil and metal ruler
- craft knife
- eraser
- 5 x 10cm (2 x 4in) piece of textured red card
- eyelet punch (small setting)
- 5 paper roses – 2 pink, 3 white
- cocktail stick
- PVA glue
- large white feather

tip

Straighten the wire stems of the flowers before using for easy handling and to avoid them looking messy.

I Place the white card on the cutting mat. Score and fold in half.

2 On the back of the red textured card, working from the left along the short edges, draw five vertical lines at 0.5, 1.5, 2.5, 3.5 and 4.5cm (¼, ⅝, 1, 1⅜ and 1¾in). Using the smallest setting, punch three holes along each line: the first at about 1cm (⅜in) from the bottom edge, the second and third around 2cm (¾in) and about 2.5cm (1in) from the top edge.

3 Thread each flower vertically through the three holes (in at the top, out of the middle, and back in again at the bottom). Tilt the flower heads forward slightly at the top so the card doesn't bend. Alternate the colours of the flowers; trim the stalks if necessary.

4 Position the rose panel in the middle of the front of the white card and very lightly mark around the corners with the pencil. Put the panel to one side. Position the feather inside the marks and trim the quill if necessary. Apply tiny dots of glue to the feather quill with a cocktail stick and stick down.

5 Apply a thin layer of PVA glue to the back of the rose panel, avoiding the punched holes. Stick the panel down on top of the feather, using the pencil marks as a guide. Hold it down until it is secure.

GOLD &LACE

This classic combination of lace and gold is suitable for a wedding or a
golden wedding anniversary. Use lace with a pretty motif like this one
for best effect – a dense pattern will not work so well for this card.

you will need

- A5 sheet of gold card
- cutting mat
- soft pencil and metal ruler
- craft knife
- eraser
- 8cm (3⅛in) square piece of lace with flower pattern
- 8cm (3⅛in) square piece of gold paper
- adhesive tape
- 14.5 x 20cm (5¾ x 8in) piece of gold paper
- glue stick
- pearlescent or glitter glue (e.g. Buttercup AppliGlu or Bright Gold AppliGlu)

tip

Try the glue out on scrap paper before you apply it to the final card... A straight line requires a lot of practice!

1 Score and fold the card in half, gold side facing out. On the inside of the card's front panel, mark out a window 5.5cm (2¼in) high, 6.5cm (2½in) wide, 2.5cm (1in) from the top and 2cm (¾in) from the sides of the panel. Cut out the window with the craft knife, turn the card over, smoothe the cut edges, and erase any left-over pencil marks.

2 Trim the piece of lace to just larger than the window and position it face down on the inside of the card. Keeping the lace flat without stretching, carefully tape one edge of the lace to the card, so the lace pattern sits inside the window. Carefully tape down the opposite edge of the lace, and then the other edges. Do not stretch the lace.

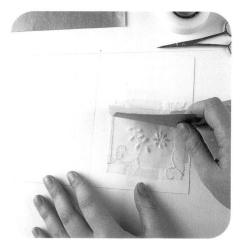

3 Tape down the square of gold paper, gold side facing down, on top of the lace panel on the inside of the card. Fold and smoothe out the fold.

4 Fold the gold inlay paper in half, gold side in. Apply glue stick to the outside of one of the panels, and glue it to the inside front of the card, over the lace and gold paper. Weigh the card down under a heavy book for at least half an hour.

5 Finally, use pearlescent or glitter glue to embellish the window frame with a combination of lines and dots (or swirls if you prefer).

PERGAMANORINGS

A special occasion warrants a special card. Use this beautiful Pergamano parchment card as an invitation to close friends, or the outer cover for a printed order of service. The golden rings and heart can be traced on the card or can feature as 3D elements glued one of top of each other.

you will need

- Pergamano parchment paper, standard size
- Pergamano Rings templates (page 76)
- adhesive tape
- metal ruler and white pencil
- mapping pen
- white 01T and gold 22T Tinta ink
- Dorso crayons, box 1
- lavender or eucalyptus oil
- kitchen paper or soft cloth
- 4-needle perforating tool
- "Excellent" perforating pad
- small ball embossing tool
- "De Luxe" embossing pad
- Perga-Soft
- 2-needle perforating tool
- Pergamano scissors
- 5-needle perforating tool
- hockeystick embossing tool
- paintbrush no. 2
- Pergakit glue
- 10 x 14cm (4 x 5½in) piece of white card

1 Trace the main template onto the parchment paper. Trace the dotted fold line, using the white pencil. Trace the scalloped heart, the petals in the corners and all the little flowers around the heart using the mapping pen and the Tinta white.

2 Trace the small dots above the heart, the central dots in the corners and the stalks using Tinta gold. Apply Dorso blue on the reverse side around the heart. Put a spot of lavender or eucalyptus oil onto a piece of kitchen paper or a soft cloth and rub over the colour gently.

3 Place the design back onto the template. Perforate the corners shallow, using the 4-needle tool.

4 With the small ball embossing tool, fully emboss the flower petals, leaves, fold line, the dots around the heart and the remaining dots in the corners. Then lightly emboss the scalloped lines along the corner outlines and the heart shape.

5 Perforate deep with the 4-needle tool. Then, with the the 2-needle tool, perforate along the scalloped outlines of the corners. Using the scissors, cut the 4-needle perforations into crosses and slits. Cut out the 2-needle perforations along the corners at the fold. Then fold the card (but not the corner decorations).

6 Attach the parchment to the template, and perforate shallow along the straight outlines with the 5-needle tool. Emboss the circle around the centre of the 5-needle perforations. Perforate again using the 5-needle tool, but deeply this time. Cut out the card along the outer holes of the 5-needle perforations.

7 Trace the 3D part of the heart with Tinta white ink. Using the 5-needle tool, perforate shallow along the heart outline. Emboss lightly along the inside of the heart with the hockeystick tool. Emboss the small circles around the central hole of the 5-needle perforations. Perforate deep along the heart outline. Cut out the heart along the outer holes.

8 Trace and paint the rings using Tinta gold ink. Using the small ball tool emboss the design and then perforate around the outside edge using the 2-needle tool. Cut out.

9 Using Pergakit glue, attach the 3D heart onto the card, then glue the rings on top of the heart.

PINK PEARL & ORGANZA

Create a beautifully old-fashioned tableau of buttons and beads in a purposefully random arrangement for a particularly evocative card. You may wish to use a different colour scheme depending on the colours in your button box.

ACETATE CONFETTI

Capture the atmosphere of the special day with a sprinkling of confetti. You could use the colour scheme of the bride and bridesmaids, or simply bright or pastel colours with gold or silver.

you will need

- hole punch
- variety of scraps of coloured paper in vibrant colours combined with silver or gold
- A4 sheet of white textured card
- cutting mat
- soft pencil and metal ruler
- craft knife
- 4.5cm (1¾in) square of scrap card
- eraser
- 2 pieces of acetate, 5cm (2in) square
- 10.5 x 20cm (4¼ x 8in) sheet of translucent yellow paper
- adhesive tape
- glue stick or PVA glue
- tweezers

tip

When sticking the confetti to the front of the card, use tweezers to pick up the confetti and a cocktail stick to apply tiny dots of PVA glue.

1 Remove the bottom of your hole punch and punch out the confetti from the scraps of coloured paper. Put them to one side.

2 With the card textured-side down, working from the right, measure and mark along the longest edges, top and bottom, at 10cm (4in) and 20cm (8in). Then score vertically between the marks and fold inwards.

3 When folded in, the left-hand panel stops just short of the next fold – this is the inside front of the card. With the left-hand panel folded in, turn the card textured-side up. Position the square of scrap card equidistant from the left, right and top edges and mark out the corners. Carefully but firmly cut out the window through both layers of card.

4 Open out the card and place textured-side down. Position one piece of acetate squarely over the window in the middle panel. Sprinkle confetti on to the acetate, place the second piece of acetate on top and carefully tape down the edges. The tape must not be visible from the front of the card.

5 Position the translucent paper on the right-hand panel, with a small flap overlapping the fold line of the card. Tape down the flap. Apply glue stick to the left-hand panel and fold it over onto the central panel. Fold over the translucent paper, then close the card. Glue extra confetti to the front, and weigh the card down under a heavy book.

WEDDING CAKE

A beautiful and elegant card, this is perfect for sending as a wedding invitation, a "keep the date" card, or as a thank-you card. You could cut the cake from gold or silver paper instead.

you will need

- A4 sheet of handmade petal paper
- cutting mat
- soft pencil and metal ruler
- craft knife
- A4 sheet of lilac plain paper
- Wedding Cake template (page 75)
- glue stick
- small piece of gold paper
- needle
- metallic gold embroidery thread
- A5 sheet of white card
- eraser

tip

You can also achieve the sewing effect by drawing dotted lines with gold or silver pen.

1 On the reverse of the handmade petal paper, lightly mark out a rectangle approximately 6 x 8cm (2⅜ x 3⅛in), then carefully tear along the marked lines. This will form the background for the wedding cake design.

2 Using the template, draw out the wedding cake on a piece of the lilac paper. Carefully cut out the cake using the craft knife and cutting mat.

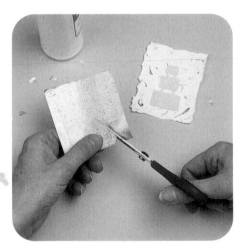

3 Glue the cake slightly lower than central onto the handmade petal paper. With the scissors, cut out a small heart from the gold paper. Glue in position on the petal paper at the top of the cake.

4 Faintly pencil the design from the template onto the cake shape, outlining each layer of the cake and adding swirls inside, then make evenly spaced holes with the needle before sewing. Using the needle with the gold thread, work along the swirls and edges of the cake in running stitch.

5 Taking the white card, score and fold it in half. Position the collage neatly on the front of the card and glue in place. Erase all remaining pencil marks.

CHAMPAGNE OCCASION

This fun card is perfect for anyone who loves champagne or music, or both! Holographic bubbles capture the sparkle of the day and this card will still be standing at the end of the evening…

you will need

- holographic card with bubble pattern
- Champagne Occasion template (page 74)
- craft knife
- sharp pair of scissors
- 12 x 36cm (4¾ x 14¼in) piece of lavender card
- cutting mat
- soft pencil and metal ruler
- eraser
- glue stick or PVA glue
- double-sided foam tape
- silver daubing stick or stamp pad
- champagne glasses stamp
- musical notes stamp
- silver pen

tip

Be careful when cutting out the cork shape – it is not easy to do. Use a sharp pair of scissors if you are not confident with the craft knife.

1 Lay the holographic card pattern-side down, and use the template to mark out three bottle shapes on the back. Carefully cut out the shapes using the craft knife.

2 Take the lavender card and, working from the left, mark along the long edges, top and bottom, at 12cm (4¾in) and 24cm (9½in), then score. Erase the pencil marks.

3 Draw a line down the middle of the left-hand panel, 6cm (2⅜in) from the left edge of the card. Position the bottle template at an angle on the line, approximately in the middle between the top and bottom edge of the card. Draw around the bottle.

4 Cut out the bottle shape to the right of the drawn line only, then erase all pencil lines. Turn the card over, face down. Mark top and bottom at 6cm (2⅜in) from the edge of the panel with the bottle cut-out, draw vertically between the marks and score along the line, above and below the edge of the cut-out bottle only. Fold along this score line, leaving the bottle shape flat.

5 Turn the card over again and fold it along the next score line so that the bottle shape sticks out over the middle panel and points to the right. Draw around the bottle shape, then cut out with the craft knife as before.

6 Fold the card out and lay face down. Measure and mark halfway across the middle panel, in the same way as before, and score above and below the bottle shape, then fold, leaving the bottle shape flat. Turn over as before and fold along the next (and final) score line to create a concertina fold.

7 Using the second bottle shape as a template, lightly mark out the position of the third bottle on the final panel, but do not cut out.

8 Apply glue stick to two of the cut-out bottle shapes and stick them precisely on the cut-out shapes on the card. Weigh down for at least 10 minutes under a heavy book.

9 Cut a narrow piece of double-sided foam tape for the neck and a wider piece for the belly of the remaining holographic bottle shape. Stick them to the back of the bottle shape, peel off the backing tape and position where marked on the final right-hand panel. Erase any remaining pencil marks.

10 Ink the stamps, then stamp glasses and musical notes all over the card, leaving space for your own message on the right-hand panel. With the silver pen, draw little scrolls and extra bubbles for the champagne glasses.

extras

Cut out another champagne bottle to decorate a matching envelope or a gift tag, made from a 9cm (3½in) square piece of card, folded in half. Alternatively, simply use the champagne glass stamp to decorate the gift tag.

ORGANZA **CONFETTI** BAG

Reminiscent of favours with its use of delicate silvery organza, this special card carries a
bag to keep and cherish, filled with wedding confetti, small sweets or a special message.
You may wish to pick a different colour scheme for a different effect.

you will need

- 10 x 22cm (4 x 8¾in) strip of silver organza ribbon
- needle (beading if necessary)
- silver thread
- pale turquoise seed beads and sequins
- cotton bud (optional)
- eyelet punch
- 8 eyelets (0.5cm (¼in) diameter used here)
- 12 x 48cm (4¾ x 19in) piece of turquoise textured handmade paper or thin card
- cutting mat
- soft pencil and metal ruler
- craft knife
- eraser
- 50cm (19¾in) length of 0.5cm (¼in) wide pale turquoise ribbon
- glue stick
- 11 x 23cm (4⅜ x 9in) piece of silver inlay paper
- confetti, sweets or the message of your choice

1 Fold the length of organza in half, smoothe the fold, then unfold. On one half, sew on the sequins and beads in a pyramid pattern: three in the bottom row, two in the middle row, one at the top. Sew through the organza, through the sequin, then through the bead, back through the sequin and organza. Tie a knot at the back of each sequin and trim the ends.

2 Fold the strip of organza the other way so the beads are on the inside. Starting at the folded end, sew up along one side about 0.5cm (¼in) from the edge in a simple running stitch, then back down again, and use an oversewing stitch to secure the edges. Tie a knot with the thread ends at the bottom and trim. Repeat on the other side.

3 Turn the bag inside out, carefully turning out the corners at the bottom (with a cotton bud, for example), and smoothe along the sewn edges. Turn in the top 2.5cm (1in) of the open end and smoothe the folds.

4 Use the eyelet punch to make four evenly spaced holes (about 2cm (¾in) apart) both on the back and the front of the turnover at the top, about 2cm (¾in) from the edge. Make sure that you apply the correct size punch for the eyelets you're going to use (the bigger size in this case).

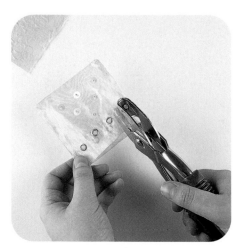

5 Change the eyelet punch accessories, insert the eyelets into the holes in the organza bag (pretty side facing out!) and fix them in place.

6 With the card texture-side down, working from the left, mark along the long edges, top and bottom, at 12cm (4¾in), 24cm (9½in) and 36cm (14¼in), and score. Erase all the pencil marks that are left.

7 Using the punch tool of the eyelet punch, make two holes in the middle of the second panel approximately 2cm (¾in) apart, and approximately 2cm (¾in) from the top edge (i.e. as far as the eyelet punch will reach). Insert the eyelets (pretty side facing out).

8 Thread the ribbon through the eyelets in the card so that both ends of the ribbon hang out at the front. Tie a double knot about 1cm (⅜in) below the eyelets, then thread the ribbon ends through the eyelets of the bag, one to the right, the other to the left, starting at the back.

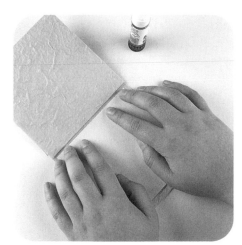

9 Glue down both inside panels using the glue stick. Fold the inlay paper in half, apply a thin line of glue next to the fold line and glue in position to the right of the central fold.

10 Fill the bag with confetti, wrapped sweets or simply a message of your choice, tie and make a neat bow at the front.

extras

For a matching gift tag, cut a 5 x 10cm (2 x 4in) piece of card and inlay paper and fold both in half to make a square tag. Sew a single sequin and bead to the front using the technique described in step 1. Glue in the inlay, hole-punch one corner and thread with ribbon.

NET & WEDDING CONFETTI

Think of a wedding and your first thoughts might be confetti, rings and the bride's veil. This collage combines all these elements to make a beautiful card to keep – vividly reminiscent of the big day for the happy couple!

you will need

- 15 x 30cm (6 x 12in) piece of white card
- cutting mat
- soft pencil and metal ruler
- craft knife and scissors
- eraser
- clear all-purpose adhesive
- cream or pink net, approximately 30cm (12in) square
- 2 imitation gold wedding rings (available through party and bridal catering shops)
- spatula
- PVA glue
- confetti
- gold stars and bells

tip

Present the card in a silver, gold or brightly coloured envelope.

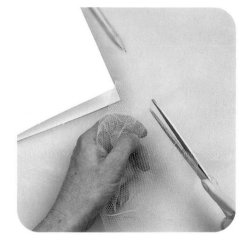

1 Taking the white card, measure halfway along the long edges, top and bottom, then score and fold. Erase all the pencil lines that are left. Cut the net fabric to approximately twice the size of the card to allow for gathering.

2 Spread clear glue all over the front of the card. Gather the net fabric and gently press it in place on the card until the glue is dry. Trim off the excess net from around the edges, taking care not to cut into the card.

3 Interlock the wedding rings or place them side by side. Dot with glue using a spatula and place on top of the net in the middle of the card. Hold in place until the glue is dry.

4 Dot a little PVA glue on the back of the confetti pieces. Place them, glue side down, on the net, so that it looks as though they have been loosely scattered onto it.

5 Glue stars and gold bells in place in the same way, spacing them evenly to give the card a balanced composition.

PETAL PAPER WALLET

Handmade petal paper and matching ribbon is all you need for this pretty card,
which is ideal for concealing a cheque or banknotes.

you will need

- 21 x 39cm (8¼ x 15⅜in) piece of petal card
- cutting mat
- soft pencil and metal ruler
- craft knife
- 11 x 20cm (4⅜ x 8in) piece of pale yellow translucent paper
- eraser
- 60cm (23½in) length of 1.5cm (⅝in) wide yellow ribbon
- small round shape, approximately 2cm (¾in) in diameter (e.g. the cap of a glue stick or the inside of a roll of tape)
- sharp scissors
- glue stick or double-sided tape

tip

To show off the petal paper card, send it in a transparent envelope.

1 Lay the petal card petal-side down on the cutting mat. Working from the left, along the long edges, mark top and bottom at just under 10cm (4in), just under 20cm (8in) and just under 30cm (12in), then score vertically between the marks.

2 Mark the middle and the right-hand score lines at 8.5cm (3⅜in) and just over 10cm (4in) from the top edge. Make a 1.5cm (⅝in) cut along both score lines between these two marks – this is where the ribbon will pass through.

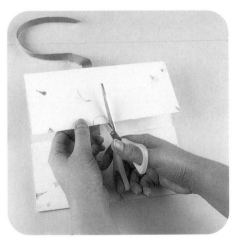

3 To prepare the inlay, mark a 1.5cm (⅝in) strip along the long edge of the translucent paper, score and fold. Erase all pencil marks. Cut the ends of the ribbon at an angle to form a point.

4 With the card petal-side down, fold inwards along all the fold lines. Unfold, then thread the ribbon from the petal side of the card to the inside and back out again.

5 Fold in the right-hand panel (which is slightly shorter). At the point on the panel edge where the ribbon runs at 90° to it, centre the glue stick cap or other round shape on the edge, draw a half circle around it, and cut it out.

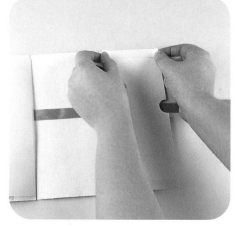

6 Apply glue to the inside of the narrow folded strip of the inlay and glue it to the underside of the far edge of the left-hand panel, taking care to leave equal margins at the top and bottom. Weigh down under a heavy book for at least 10 minutes.

7 Apply glue or double-sided tape along the top, bottom and far left edges of the left-hand panel and fold over. Apply double-sided tape along the top and bottom edges only of the right-hand panel and stick down. Weigh down again under a heavy book.

8 Adjust the ribbon and tie a bow at approximately two thirds of the width of the card (i.e. if the ribbon is 60cm (24in) long, it should be 3cm (1¼in) longer sticking out on the left than on the right-hand side of the card).

variations

For a simpler way to secure what's inside your card, try winding very thin ribbon in a zig-zag pattern around the whole card. A combination of expensive ribbon and textured card is beautiful in itself.

POP-UP CAKE

Stylishly simple but stunningly effective, this card is more about what's inside than out. A classy wedding greeting that can also be adapted for other cake occasions.

you will need

- 13.5 x 36cm (5¼ x 14¼in) piece of textured white card
- cutting mat
- soft pencil and metal ruler
- craft knife
- eraser
- pearlescent white or champagne-coloured paper
- Fiskars heart border punch or similar
- tweezers
- PVA glue
- cocktail stick
- glue stick

tip

Try brightly coloured translucent, neon or sparkly holographic paper as a funky alternative to the pearlescent paper used for the cake borders.

1 Place card textured-side down on the cutting mat. From the right, measure and mark along the long edges, top and bottom, at 9cm (3½in), 18cm (7in), and just under 27cm (10¾in), and score along these lines.

2 Along the bottom edge, measure and mark at 4, 3 and 2cm (1½, 1¼, and ¾in) on either side of the left-hand score line. Turn the card 90°. From the bottom edge, parallel to the score line, measure and mark at 9cm (3½in) from the 2cm (¾in) marks, 6.5cm (2½in) from the 3cm (1¼in) marks and 3.5cm (1⅜in) from the 4cm (1½in) marks.

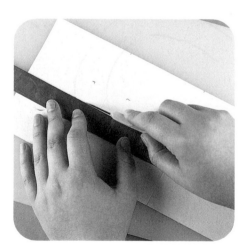

3 Line up the ruler between the two marks that are 4cm (1½in) apart and 9cm (3½in) from the bottom edge, and carefully cut between them, ensuring the score line is at a 90° angle to the cut. In the same way, cut between the other two pairs of marks that are 6cm (2⅜in) and 8cm (3⅛in) apart. These will form the tiers of the cake.

4 Line up the ruler between one end of the 4cm (1½in) wide cut and the corresponding mark at the bottom edge of the card. Starting from the end of the cut, carefully score down only as far as the cut below. Repeat for the other end of the 4cm (1½in) wide cut, then repeat the process for the 6cm (2⅜in) and 8cm (3⅛in) wide cuts.

5 On the third panel of the card, measure and mark an 8cm (3⅛in) wide horizontal line, 7cm (2¾in) from the top edge of the card and 0.5cm (¼in) from the panel edges, then cut along it with the craft knife. Erase any pencil lines that are left.

6 Practise using the punch, then punch out several continuous lengths of heart border from the pearlescent paper. Keep the resulting heart cut-outs.

7 Cut one strip of heart border just under 8cm (3⅛in) in length and three strips of just under 4cm (1½in), 6cm (2⅜in) and 8cm (3⅛in) respectively. Fold each of the strips in half first to make sure that the pattern is evenly balanced.

8 With the card flat and the cake tiers on the right, glue the heart cut-outs to the left of the wedding cake, using tweezers and dots of PVA glue applied with a cocktail stick.

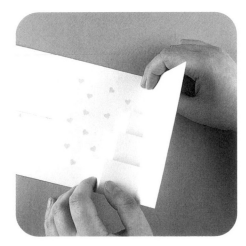

9 Carefully manipulate the scored tiers of the cake to fold inwards, while the remaining bit of fold line at the top folds out. Fold this section completely, pressing down to smoothe the fold lines of the cake.

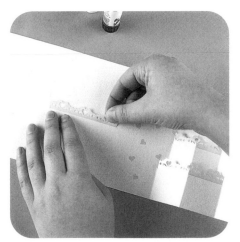

10 Apply glue stick to the front bottom edge of the border strips and attach them to the inside edges of the corresponding cake tiers. Apply glue stick to the front bottom edge of the long strip for the front of the card and slip it through the long cut. Weigh down under a heavy book for at least 10 minutes.

11 Fold the outside of the card around the inside to hide the cut-out area. Apply glue only to the open inside edges of the card, then match the corners up. Fold the card up completely and weigh down under a heavy book for half an hour.

TEMPLATES

The templates shown here are actual size.
They may be easily enlarged or reduced on
a photocopier if you wish to make a larger
or smaller card.

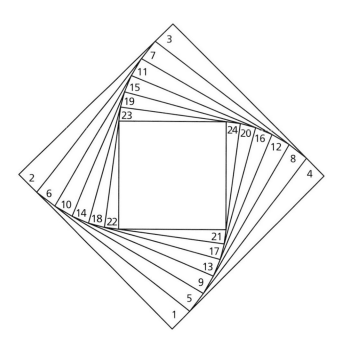

The Happy Couple
(page 24)

Triple Heart Concertina
(page 32)

Champagne Occasion
(page 60)

Wedding Cake
(page 58)

Cherubs & Hearts
(page 44)

Pergamano Rings (main,
3D heart, rings)
(page 50)

Embossed Heart
(page 38)

Woven Ribbon
(page 17)

Pergamano Hearts
(page 40)

SUPPLIERS

United Kingdom

Art and Crafts Direct
Unit 44, Coney Green Business Park
Wingfield View, Claycross
Derbyshire S45 9JW
Tel: 01246 252 313
www.artsandcraftsdirect.com
General craft supplier.

Blade Rubber Stamps Ltd.
12 Bury Place
London WC1A 2JL
Tel: 020 7831 4123
Email: info@bladerubberstamps.co.uk
www.bladerubberstamps.co.uk
*Suppliers of stamps, border punches,
embossing powders, etc.*

Cornelissen & Son Ltd.
105 Great Russell Street
London WC1B 3RY
Tel: 020 7636 1045
General craft supplier.

Cowling & Wilcox
26–28 Broadwick Street
London W1F 8HX
Tel: 020 7734 9557
www.cowlingandwilcox.com
Email: art@cowlingandwilcox.com
General craft supplier.

Craft Creations
Ingersoll House
Delamare Road, Cheshunt
Hertfordshire EN8 9ND
Tel: 01992 781 900
Email: enquiries@craftcreations.com
www.craftcreations.com
General craft supplier.

Cranberry Card Company
Unit 4, Greenway Workshops
Bedwas House Industrial Estate
Bedwas, Caerphilly CF83 8DW
Tel: 02920 807 941
Email: info@cranberrycards.co.uk
www.cranberrycards.co.uk
Selection of card, paper and accessories.

Creative Crafts
11 The Square
Winchester
Hampshire SO23 9ES
Tel: 01962 856266
Email: sales@creativecrafts.co.uk
www.creativecrafts.co.uk
General craft supplier.

The English Stamp Company
Worth Matravers, Dorset
BH19 3JP
Tel: 01929 439 117
Email: sales@englishstamp.com
www.englishstamp.com
*Suppliers of stamps, paints, inkpads and
handmade paper. Mail-order only.*

Falkiner Fine Papers Ltd.
76 Southampton Row
London WC1B 4AR
Tel: 020 7831 1151
*Carries a large range of handmade papers.
Also offers a mail-order service.*

Fiskars Brands UK Ltd.
Brackla Industrial Estate
Bridgend
Mid Glamorgan CF31 2XA
01656 655 595
anthonyl@fiskars.demon.co.uk
and:
Richard Sankey & Ltd.
Bennerly Road
Nottingham NG6 8PE
0115 927 7335
info@rsankey.co.uk
Wide range of craft equipment.

Homecrafts Direct
Unit 2, Wanlip Road
Syston
Leicester LE7 1PD
Tel: 0116 269 7733
www.homecrafts.co.uk
Email: info@homecrafts.co.uk
*Mail-order service. Selection of handmade
papers and range of craft products.*

John Lewis
Oxford Street
London W1A 1EX
Tel: 020 7629 7711
www.johnlewis.com
General range of craft materials.

Paperchase
Flagship Store and Main Office
213 Tottenham Court Road
London W1T 7PS
Tel: 020 7467 6200
*Retailers of stationery, wrapping paper and art
materials. Call for your nearest outlet.*
Mail order tel: 0161 839 1500
www.paperchase.co.uk
Email: mailorder@paperchase.co.uk

T N Lawrence
208 Portland Road
Hove
East Sussex
BN3 5QT
Tel: 01273 260 260
www.lawrence.co.uk
*Carries a large range of papers as well as
general artist's materials.*

The Stencil Store
41a Heronsgate Road
Chorleywood
Hertfordshire
WD3 5BL
Tel: 01923 285 577
Email: stencilstore@onetel.com
www.stencilstore.com
*Supply wide range of stencil designs. Phone for
nearest store or to order catalogue.*

VV Rouleaux
6 Marylebone High Street
London W1M 3PB
Tel: 020 7224 5179
Fax: 020 7224 5193
Email: marylebone@vvrouleaux.com
www.vvrouleaux.com
*Huge selection of ribbons, trimmings,
feathers, fabric and paper flowers.*

Australia

Artwise Amazing Paper
186 Enmore Road
Enmore
NSW 2042
Tel: 02 9519 8237
www.amazingpaper.com.au

Lincraft
www.lincraft.com.au
General craft supplier. Stores throughout
Australia.

Myer Centre, Rundle Mall
Adelaide, SA 5000
Tel: 02 8231 6611

Myer Centre, Queen Street
Brisbane, QLD 4000
Tel: 07 3221 0064

Shop D02/D03
Canberra Centre
Bunda Street
Canberra, ACT 2601
Tel: 02 6257 4516

Australia on Collins
Melbourne, VIC 3000
Tel: 03 9650 1609

Imperial Arcade, Pitt Street
Sydney, NSW 2000
Tel: 02 9221 5111

Paper Fantasy
256a Charters Towers Road
Hermit Park, QLD 4812
Tel: 07 4725 1272

Paperwright
124 Lygon Street
Carlton, VIC 3053
Tel: 03 9663 8747

Spotlight
Tel: 1800 656 256
www.spotlight.com.au
General craft supplier. Call for nearest store.

South Africa

Art Shop
140a Victoria Avenue
Benoni West 1503
Tel/Fax: 011 421 1030

Arts, Crafts and Hobbies
72 Hibernia Street
George 6529
Tel/Fax: 044 874 1337
Mail-order service available.

Pen and Art
Shop 313, Musgrave Centre
Musgrave Road
Durban 4001
Tel/Fax: 031 201 0094

Bowker Arts and Crafts
52 4th Avenue
Newton Park
Port Elizabeth 6001
Tel: 041 365 2487
Fax: 041 365 5306

Centurion Kuns
Shop 45, Eldoraigne Shopping Mall
Saxby Road
Eldoraigne 0157
Tel/Fax: 012 654 0449

Crafty Supplies
Shop UG 2, Stadium on Main
Main Road, Claremont 7700
Cape Town
Tel: 021 671 0286
Fax: 021 671 0308

Creative Papercraft
64 Judd Street
Horizon 1724
Tel/Fax: 011 763 5682

L & P Stationery and Art
141 Zastron Street
Westdene
Bloemfontein 9301
Tel: 051 430 1085
Fax: 051 430 4102

Le Papier du Port
Gardens Centre
Cape Town 8000
Tel: 021 462 4796
Fax: 021 461 9281
Mail-order service available.

New Zealand

Brush & Palette
50 Lichfield Street
Christchurch
Tel/Fax: 03 366 3088

Fine Art Papers
200 Madras Street
Christchurch
Tel: 03 379 4410
Fax: 03 379 4443

Gordon Harris Art Supplies
4 Gillies Avenue
Newmarket, Auckland
Tel: 09 520 4466
Fax: 09 520 0880
and:
31 Symonds Street
Auckland Central
Tel: 09 377 9992

Littlejohns
170 Victoria Street
Wellington
Tel: 04 385 2099
Fax: 04 385 2090

Studio Art Supplies
81 Parnell Rise
Parnell, Auckland
Tel: 09 377 0302
Fax: 09 377 7657

G Webster & Co Ltd.
44 Manners Street
Wellington
Tel: 04 384 2134
Fax: 04 384 2968

INDEX